Cabbage ar

Memories of a 1950s Childhood

Cathy Murray

To Rose

My mother-in-law, Rose Murray, lived until she was ninety eight years old. We often encouraged Rose to write her life's story. She was born in 1908 and, as she frequently reminded us, had lived through two world wars in the heart of London's East End. Aged about ninety two Rose started to record her memories but it was too late. She couldn't sustain the interest or the concentration; all she managed to capture was a short memoir about her childhood.

Rose's memoir is a fascinating document and it's such a pity that we didn't help her to write more of her reminiscences while she was able.

For many years I've been interested in family history. I've explored the twists and turns of most of the branches of our family tree. Reading Rose's memoir and thinking about her story made me decide that I would record some of my own recollections while I still could.

I've dedicated Cabbage and Semolina to Rose, the inspiration for this book.

Why Cabbage and Semolina?

If you're wondering why I've called this book Cabbage and Semolina then you definitely didn't go to primary school in Britain in the 1950s. Everyone had either to stay for school dinners or go home to eat. There were no packed lunches or going out to the chippy in those days. I know every generation complains about school dinners but in the 1950s they really were bad. If Cabbage was on the menu it was chopped and cooked, stalks and all, until it came out onto the plate as a gritty, lumpy, stringy mush which you had to eat whether you liked it or not.

Of course, once the main dish of the day was eaten your reward was offered. Pudding!

Baked suet and treacle roll; stewed fruit crumble; chocolate sponge; pink sponge; jam sponge; stewed fruit pie, all served with custard: fluorescent yellow, thick and glutinous. In summer for our puddings we had jelly, trifle, cold stewed fruit, ice-cream (once), cold custard. And at any time of year, Semolina: vanilla, chocolate, pink, and sometimes with cold stewed fruit added for an extra treat. If you look at a bowl of wallpaper paste and a bowl of semolina there's not much difference but we ate it anyway.

Our school dinners were served in a long, low room known as the canteen with serving hatches opening off one side to the kitchen. The walls of the canteen were painted a murky cream at the top and dark green downwards from dado height. These walls ran with water during the winter months when the warmth from the kitchen, the food and the bodies of a couple of hundred hungry school kids formed rivulets of condensation. There was no actual heating in the canteen so the food quickly cooled and coagulated becoming ever less appetising.

Our all-time least favourite school dinner was baked liver. The liver wasn't served with onions in the traditional manner but was dished up solo, it's burnished, metallic flavour slightly obscured by the thick, solidifying Oxo gravy dolloped on top. Accompanied by the school canteen's signature dish of lumpy mashed potato, this fortnightly staple was dreaded.

There was no choice; not even take it or leave it. You had to have a portion of everything and you had to eat the lot. And the formidable dinner ladies made sure that every last scrap on your plate was eaten.

But once, on Liver Day, a temeritous boy named Michael said, "No! I don't want any liver."

"Eat your liver," was the determined response uttered several times by the dinner lady until Michael, in a fit of bravado, picked up the offending offal and flung it with considerable force across the room.

"I don't like liver," shouted Michael as he jumped up from his place at the table. "I'm not eating any of it."

"You little b-- bad boy! Where d'you think you're going? Get back here NOW!" as Michael fled the room.

Eat it all up or live to regret it was the 1950s way with school dinners.

My younger sister and I sometimes went home for dinner but the difficulty was a serious lack of time. We only had one hour to walk home, eat the meal our mum had cooked and walk back to school before the bell rang and all the classes lined up in regimental ranks in the playground. As the crow flew we could arrive home in five minutes but there was a busy railway line between the school and our house with no crossing point so we had to go the long way round. If we were lucky the teacher would end the class a minute or two early and we could actually be on our way home when the "twelve o'clock buzzer" sounded to announce the dinner break at a nearby factory.

We had to walk briskly home and back again if we were to have any chance of being in the playground line on time. There wasn't a spare minute for dawdling or playing the fool. So we preferred staying at school for dinner to avoid the worry of being back late even though we hated the food. One time the meat was so tough and full of gristle my younger sister kept it in her mouth all afternoon and only spat it out when we got home.

Nylon Frocks and Cotton Socks

All our clothes, except coats and undies, were home-made by our mother who was a dab-hand with her sewing machine. She had a Singer sewing machine purchased in 1953 for £22 / 18s / 9d. How do I know that? My dad saved the receipt (in case the machine didn't work and he had to take it back to the shop) and I've still got it in my family history box.

Mum sewed dresses for winter and for summer; shorts for going on holiday; and blouses for school. She knitted cardigans, jumpers, gloves, scarves; hats; even a woolly swimsuit.

Note: no trousers. Girls didn't wear trousers in those days.

We had new best clothes for Christmas and new best clothes at Whitsun; and then the old best clothes became our school clothes. It wasn't that it was make-do-and-mend anymore: it's just that the habits of the wartime years had stuck with our mum. She would still make us unravel an old jumper and re-wind the wool so she could knit it up again.

Usually the clothes our mum created were sensible, hard-wearing and made from natural fibres. But when I was about six years old and invited to be the chief bridesmaid at my auntie's wedding I got the dress of a life-time. Pink (naturally) with tiny, deeper pink flowers sprigged all over the fabric; gathered in at the waist into a full skirt; a matching pink satin sash tied round the middle into a big bow at the back; and two sticking out petticoats underneath that gave it the typical fifties look. And, it was made out of nylon.

Invented in the U.S.A. in the late 1930s and used extensively throughout World War Two for military purposes (parachutes and nylon stockings come to mind), nylon hit the fashion headlines in the mid-fifties. The new wonder fabric: easily washed; non-iron; stylish and bang on trend.

Nylon frocks! All little girls wanted a nylon frock and I was no exception. My bridesmaid dress and co-ordinating bouquet were a delight. It's a pity the wedding was in early April on a cold, wet, grey day and, as the nylon fabric had as much warmth as a plastic carrier bag, we bridesmaids had to wear our winter coats on top of the frocks.

Nylon fabric had a few other drawbacks. It certainly dried quickly on the washing line if the sun was shining. However, if dried indoors it was drip, drip, dry all over the floor. Once dried it turned out that the non-iron features of nylon were exaggerated. Unless you wanted the crumpled look, it definitely did need ironing. Get the iron too cool and the crumples remained; get the iron too hot and the nylon melted away in front of your eyes leaving just a sticky brown mess on the iron which hardened to an immovable lump when cold. And, of course, it was highly flammable. In an age of open coal fires and widespread cigarette smoking, domestic accidents were common-place with the inevitable consequences for the wearers of the dresses and their rescuers.

My second nylon frock was a hand-me-down from a more affluent friend-of-the-family. It was all white, mid-calf length and over-decorated. Puff sleeves which ended at the elbow with a pearl (fake I presume) encrusted cuff; a triple layer of frills around the hem; a stand-up collar with more pearls and some shiny bits as well; and an embroidery pattern of swirling flowers all over the skirt in white silk thread. I've searched Ebay and countless vintage websites looking for its sister but never seen anything like it.

My third nylon frock was actually bought from an up-market department store in Leeds. I don't remember what the occasion was but it must have been significant to have come from such a posh shop. The dress was pale turquoise with tiny white dots; a full skirt and a neat little white collar. Worn with crepe soled white sandals it looked a picture. I only wore it once because it was scorched (by my mum) with the iron and it wasn't much use after that.

We always had sandals for the summer: usually Clarks, usually brown but occasionally white; always with a T-bar; and always worn with white ankle socks.

Ankle socks in summer; knee socks in winter.

The socks were made out of cotton and to keep them sparkling white they got a boil wash and consequently they shrank in the foot and became increasingly uncomfortable.

The knee socks had elastic woven into the top to stop them falling down but that didn't last long. So you had to get a piece of knicker elastic and tie it into a loop and use it as a garter. This worked quite well unless you made the loop too tight: then your circulation stopped and your leg started going blue. Tights weren't invented until the 1960s so white, cotton socks were what we had to wear.

Goose Grease and Liberty Bodices

One Christmas my grandad turned up with a surprise. It was a goose that he wanted my mum to cook for the celebration dinner. My mum was too young; too polite; and too well brought up to say "No" and so the goose was duly stuffed and then stuffed into the oven.

Grandad was certain that the goose would be wonderful. He also explained to our mother how she could save the fat (goose grease he called it) and use it for the remainder of the winter as a preventative for colds and flu.

The goose filled the cooker. Mum was an inexperienced cook and she didn't know just how much fat was going to come off the bird until it started to flow out of the cooker all over the kitchen floor.

The floor was awash with the slippery grease and dealing with it was hardly conducive to "peace and goodwill to all men"; especially towards grandad.

Grandad was really annoyed that the fat had got away and mum was even more annoyed because her Christmas dinner plans were in ruins.

However, it was only later I realised that grandad's plans for the health preserving properties of the goose grease were meant for me and my younger sister. We were supposed to have our chests rubbed with the noxious stuff every morning before we went to school to ward off the "germs" that were waiting for us round every corner.

Eventually my mum became a master of the bacon and eggs; Shepherd's Pie; roast meat and two veg; cakes, pies and custard style of cuisine but thankfully never, ever, goose again and no greasy rubs.

With the exception of Vic of course. Vic Vapour Rub: smeared on your handkerchief; wiped round the end of your nose; rubbed on your throat and chest. Guaranteed to unblock nasal passages Vic would send you into a deep, untroubled coma. Bliss.

All through the winter we wore vests but when it was really cold, out came the liberty bodices. These were intended to provide an extra layer of insulation and they were made of a fluffy-lined cotton fabric. Unfortunately, the liberty bodices shrank in the wash (because being white they had to have a boil wash) and they bore more of a resemblance to a straight-jacket than to liberty. You had to stand with your arms upraised above your head while the liberty bodice was dragged down over your head and top half until you were encased and could hardly move let alone breathe. All through the day you felt constricted and constrained. And you were just as cold anyway because of the lack of heating in sitting rooms, class rooms, waiting rooms and bed rooms. Getting the liberty bodice off was nigh on impossible and visions of scissors and sharp knives weren't too far from reality. Eventually, after they'd been boiled to half their starting size and the fluffy-lining was matted and knotted, the liberty bodices were discarded and used for floor cloths where their absorbent properties proved excellent for cleaning up greasy floors and cookers.

11

It wasn't just grandad who was concerned with prevention rather than cure. Every day our mum gave us a spoonful of cod liver oil followed by a spoonful of rose hip syrup which were intended to make us fitter and healthier. The nauseating, tainted fishy flavour of the vitamin packed oil was supposed to be masked by the sickly, sweet vitamin enriched syrup. It wasn't. The oil and the syrup combined into a glutinous gel that stuck halfway down your throat and made you want to vomit.

At school, every day we were given a third of a pint of full fat milk. This was because each one of us was presumed to have a calcium deficiency and the milk was to make us fit and healthy. Sometimes in winter the milk froze and the solidified fat on the top of the milk would push the bottle top upwards for an inch or so. When the milk crate was brought into the classroom the frozen milk would thaw down the sides of the bottles creating a dirty, milky puddle all over the floor. On hot summer days the milk would go slightly off but we were still obliged to drink it all up through a waxed paper straw poked through the foil cap on the top of the bottle. Occasionally the supplier didn't have enough milk. To make up for the deficiency some of the same mini milk bottles were sent but they were filled with orange squash. We liked the orange squash a lot more than the milk and whoever the teacher chose to get the orange squash felt highly favoured.

Smash and Grab

At the bottom of our street was a waste ground. Naturally all of us kids went there to play as soon as we were old enough to be let out of the garden.

There was a slight incline in the street as it neared the waste ground, which we called "the tip", which gave you a bit of speed if you were on your roller skates or cadgie. If you were running you could easily trip and sprain your ankle on the rough, uneven ground where the road ended and the dereliction started.

In case you don't know, a cadgie is a set of pram wheels with an orange box fixed onto the frame to make a seat. It definitely doesn't have any brakes. You kick off at the top of a slope, scramble into the box and cling on desperately until you arrive at the bottom of the hill hoping and praying you won't be tipped out. Some kids had an extra set of wheels, a cross bar to connect the wheels together and a skipping rope for steering; and still no brakes. Although more sophisticated, this model was just as capable as the prototype of ensuring cuts, grazes, scratches, bruises and fractures.

The waste ground was bounded to the right by a main road where coal lorries went speeding past with monotonous regularity. To the left of the waste ground was a railway embankment which shielded us from the goods trains which went up and down the line at a fairly slow speed in a cloud of steam. It had that wonderfully burnished, pungent, carbon smell that you only ever encounter these days at heritage railway sites.

At the far end of the waste ground was a parade of small shops with flats above: bread shop; newsagents and sweet shop; grocery store; fish and chip shop; and the small office of a funeral director which always had an urn and a vase of dusty, white flowers in the window.

There were gardens behind the shops. The garden at the back of the shop that was nearest to the tip was bordered by a stream which flowed out from a culvert in the railway embankment. The water was usually only a few inches deep but occasionally it became a torrent if it had rained heavily the night before. Strict parental instructions told us that never, ever, under any circumstances were we to go in that culvert which of course we ignored.

We all dared each other to crawl into the culvert and most of us would go in for several yards but only the bravest and most fool-hardy went any further. Richard Williams went all the way through and shouted at us from the other side but he was the only one. Sometime later we heard there were very large rats in the culvert and none of us ever went in again. It was only a long time afterwards I realised that a wise parent had thought of a way to manage the danger without spoiling our fun.

The tip was so named for obvious reasons: all sorts of stuff got dumped there. One day we found a rusty, old tin chest containing three or four gas masks left over from the War. They had a peculiar smell. I suppose it was a mixture of damp and disinfectant and rubber and whatever other materials the gas masks were made from but someone said it was the smell of dead people. And that was it. We ran! The toughies pulled the masks over their heads and the rest of us screamed. It was probably the best game of "Chase" in the history of childhood as we hurtled over the site for the rest of the day. Twenty four hours later the gas masks were gone although the chest stayed there for longer.

We played war-games, Us and Jerry, where the boys picked sides and had fights with each other. The girls were captured and held prisoner in the den until it was time for an air battle when it was every man for himself and with arms extended we swooped around the sky dive-bombing and screaming "Ack - ack - ack" until we were tired out.

Other days it was Cowboys and Indians where the boys picked sides, had fights with each other and captured the girls. Everyone had a horse which was ridden at a lop-sided trot one hand holding the imaginary reins while the other shot the two-fingered pistol until the Sheriff called for law and order and we collapsed into the den.

The den was built within the shelter of a great mound of rubble which was covered in grass and weeds. We burrowed into the rubble and furnished the den with a couple of boxes, a broken settee and a jam jar of wild flowers. We could hide there from passers-by and from each other; use the sanctuary of the den to call out names and insults; and get some shelter from the wind and the weather.

Another great game was milk bottle smashing. In those days, most people had their daily pinta or two delivered by the milkman in returnable glass bottles with a foil cap on the top: silver for pasteurised; gold for Jersey and a metal top you removed with a bottle opener for sterilised.

If we could acquire a few bottles (which was definitely not allowed) we lined them up on a pile of bricks. Then we took turns to hurl stones at the bottles with a view to smashing them into as many tiny pieces as possible.

It was really rather difficult to hit and smash the bottles this way and so, oblivious to the danger of flying glass shards, we took our turns in throwing the bottles directly at bricks placed on the ground.

The crashing, smashing noises were such a giveaway that it wasn't long before the nearest available adult was hot-footing to the edge of the tip to yell at their off-spring:

"Get yourself back home NOW! And the rest of you - I'll tell your mams".

And they almost invariably did.

War and Peace

Although we didn't realise it at the time we were growing up in a momentous era. Our parents had survived World War Two and they were expecting the world to become a better place. Whoever they were, wherever they lived, their lives were turned upside down by their wartime experiences. No family escaped the trauma. Whether at home or abroad; on active service or in reserved occupations; working for the war-effort; attending school or just trying to feed a family; everyone was affected every day for over five years. And then the war stopped and, in 1945, there was the biggest political shake-up imaginable. The Labour Party, promising nationalisation of the major industries and the creation of a National Health Service, won a landslide majority in Parliament.

The next general election was held in 1950 and was once again won by the Labour Party. Considerable re-organisation of constituency boundaries had occurred since 1945 and Labour's massive majority of one hundred and forty five Members of Parliament was reduced to five. Even though a further one and a half million people voted Labour in 1950 most of them lived in safe Labour seats so the huge popular support for the nationalisation and health reforms that had been implemented between 1945 and 1950 did not translate into a significant parliamentary majority. After a year, hoping to increase the number of Labour M.Ps., Prime Minister Clement Atlee called another election. This time the balance of power shifted to the Conservatives although the votes cast for the Labour Party increased by a further quarter of a million. The first-past-the-post system meant that the Conservatives had a majority of sixteen M.Ps. and formed the next government.

Another election was held in 1955 in which the Conservatives increased their majority to sixty and this success was repeated in 1959. That was the year when Prime Minister Harold Macmillan made his "you've never had it so good" speech. Almost fifty per cent of the voters agreed with him and increased the Conservative majority to one hundred.

However, despite the change of political parties, the transformations post 1945 were sustained by the Conservatives throughout the decade. This was the decade which saw the Korean War; the Festival of Britain; the coronation of Queen Elizabeth II; the discovery of the structure of DNA; the start of commercial television on ITV; Burgess and Maclean; the Angry Young Men; Smog; Britain's first nuclear power station; Suez; independence from colonial rule in the Gold Coast (Ghana); Britain getting its own atomic bomb; Sputnik; and the inauguration of the motorway network. Wow!

Homes and Gardens

The post-war housing shortage meant that local councils were tasked with building more homes for families to live in. The majority of people rented their homes either from the local council or from private landlords. It was the policy of some local councils to include an offer of a council house in the remuneration package they gave to staff. This property would be available to rent for the duration of the individual's employment with the council. As a Sanitary Inspector, and later as a Meat Inspector and a Public Health Officer, my dad was one of those employees. Throughout the 1950s each time my dad changed his job we moved to a different council house.

Our first council house was in Glossop in Derbyshire. It was a lovely three bedroomed semi-detached house that was just a few years old. It had a big garden partly enclosed by dry stone walls as it was situated on the edge of the countryside. There's a photograph of the house in my family history box. On the photograph the house looks light and airy with a lawned front garden. As my parents were only in their twenties and recently married, they didn't have much furniture and they couldn't afford carpets. My dad made some rugs. He bought a canvas backing which had match head sized holes in it. Through this he pulled short lengths of wool using a special tool that magically twisted the woollen tufts into place. One rug, which was plain and fawn in colour, was positioned in front of the fireplace in the sitting room. This was probably his practice piece because the next rug my dad made was much more complicated. It was intended for my bedroom and this rug had a white sheep in the centre with some sprigs of green for grass at the sheep's feet and a pink border. It was lovely and accompanied us from house to house for many years.

My mum and dad had saved up and bought for their own bedroom a wooden bed frame, matching dressing table, chest of drawers and a wardrobe. In my bedroom, in addition to the rug, I just had a cot and a bookcase which my dad had made when he was at school. It was painted white and was slightly lop-sided but he'd done his best. My mum made curtains on her sewing machine for all the rooms. One of my dad's aunts donated us a second-hand dining table and chairs. In the kitchen there was an electric cooker and, pride of place, an electric washing machine. The washing machine was just a single drum with a mangle mounted on it which, for storage, folded away inside the drum.

The washing was agitated inside the drum for several minutes and then mum had to drain out the soapy water, re-fill the drum with clear water and let it agitate again. After the rinsing water was drained away the wet residue was squeezed out of the washing by passing it through the mangle. The mangle was turned by hand, it wasn't an electric one, and despite the claims of the manufacturers, washing day was still hard work. We didn't have a fridge but mostly that didn't matter because food was bought as it was needed and used on the same day. Except, that is, in the summer when milk could go off even within one day. So, to try and slow down the souring process the bottle of milk was stored on the kitchen window sill in a jug of cold water.

After a couple of years my dad got a new job and we moved into a new-build, three bedroomed semi on a large council estate on the outskirts of Wakefield. The estate was still being built and we were one of the first families to live there. Behind the house were open fields bordering a country lane. The houses were built on a bit of a slope and there were steps from the front garden down a banking to the road in front of the houses. The steps were steep and little legs frequently fell down them. At first the garden was just rough soil until my dad dug it all over and planted potatoes, front and back. This was "to do the soil good" and after a year he flattened the back garden with a roller and planted grass. Meanwhile, we were happy enough to sit in the dirt with a couple of spoons and a pot of water and mix up soil and water to make "odgy-podgy". That was until my slightly younger sister started eating the soil and the game came to a sudden end when she threw up all over herself.

Two years later: new job; new house.

Only it wasn't a new house at all. It was another three bedroomed semi but it had been built in the 1920s. The windows were much smaller and the house was considerably darker than the others. The house was made even more gloomy because the walls of the passage from the front door were panelled in sheets of polished wood veneer. The window in the front door was set with a stained glass design which cast coloured lights onto the floor if the sun ever shone but usually just made the passage even darker. And there was a large, loud-ticking, grandfather clock. By now my grandma, my dad's mum, had died and Goose Grease Grandad had moved into a small prefab so most of his furniture had been passed onto us, including the grandfather clock. The grandfather clock terrified me because it had a man-in-the-moon painted on the panel behind the clock face which seemed to be looking at you wherever you went along the passage. Upstairs or downstairs moon-man's gaze followed you. Combined with the pendulum's tick-tock and the cavernous cabinet which housed it the grandfather clock was an oppressive, looming presence.

This house was different to the other houses because it had a front room, a back sitting room and tiny scullery kitchen whereas each of the newly built houses had a sitting room and a large dining kitchen. There was a fire place in each room in this new, old house and every one was badly needed as the house was draughty and had poor insulation. Of course, there was no central heating and in the winter we would huddle round the coal fire in the back room trying to keep warm. On winter nights we took a hot-water bottle to bed and dived in under the blankets fully clothed until the bed was warm enough to change into our nighties. The next day the windows were often iced up on the interior and, if the house ever warmed up, the ice thawed into puddles on the window sill.

One night the wind was storm force and it blew the slates off the roof of the house on the opposite side of the road. The slates came flying straight through our front bedroom windows. The glass shattered into countless shards, some sharply pointed and over a foot long. These were flung into the room and impaled into the bed. Fortunately my mum and dad weren't in bed at the time but were sitting with us children in the under stairs cupboard waiting for the storm to blow itself out.

Every house in the street had a small back garden. There was just enough space for a garden shed, a vegetable patch and a square of grass to play on. A washing line went from a hook on the back wall of the house to a pole at the bottom of the garden. Washing day was a brilliant white billowing of sheets, pillow cases and towels until a few of the steam trains on the railway line behind the houses opposite had passed by. After that the spattering of sooty dots was sometimes so great that the washing had to be done again.

We lived in this house until we moved to Lincolnshire in 1962 when my dad got another promotion and changed his job again.

Tonsils and Adenoids

The National Health Service actually started in 1948 when the Labour Government, determined that its post-war reconstruction would address the five giant evils of want, disease, squalor, ignorance and idleness. Labour ensured that in the future there would be good healthcare for all. The Labour Health Minister, Aneurin Bevan, decided that hospitals, doctors, nurses, pharmacists, opticians and dentists would be brought together within one umbrella organisation to provide services that would be free for all at the point of delivery. The healthcare of the nation was organised on a massive scale during the War and this had demonstrated what could be done if there was the political will to make it happen. The core principle was that the new health service would be available to everyone and financed entirely out of taxation which would ensure that people paid in according to their income. However this principle was watered down in 1952 when prescription charges of one shilling were introduced; there was also a one pound payment for dental treatment although hospitals and doctors remained free to visit.

Nearly everyone I know who grew up in the 1950s went to an N.H.S. hospital and had their tonsils removed; and if they were extra unlucky their adenoids came out too. Did anyone actually know what tonsils were for other than causing tonsillitis? And apart from making you talk down your nose, what was the point of adenoids?

Apparently they're both part of the immune system and the tonsils function to trap bacteria but if they're not there it doesn't really matter, so that's good news!

What wasn't good news was the way in which the operation was undertaken in the early 1950s. I was just five years old when I had my tonsils out. I had to go onto an adult ward; my mother was sent away and not allowed to return for two days; I was kept in hospital (on the adult ward) for five days during which time only my mother (no other family members) was allowed to look and wave at me through a glass partition at the other end of the room. Then on day five she was allowed onto the ward to get me ready to take home and the nurses told her to give me ice-cream every day.

Can you imagine if children were treated like that in hospital these days? There would be uproar and rightly too.

After I recovered from the tonsils operation I started biting my nails. I'd never done this before the hospitalisation and it's remained a lifelong habit although I usually manage to control it. My mother, not a person who willingly helped anyone out with excuses, was convinced it was the trauma of separation that caused the habit and I'm sure she was right. I can so vividly remember the experience and the feelings of abandonment: although not in those words, of course.

Fortunately, I didn't have to go into hospital again for a very long time; I still continued to have the symptoms of tonsillitis even though the tonsils had gone; and apart from the nail biting, I don't suppose the experience did me much harm.

When my youngest sister went to hospital for her tonsillectomy about fifteen years later she went onto a dedicated children's ward. Her mum was able to stay with her for most of the time and she was only in hospital over-night. Much better!

Rhubarb and Fillings

During the War (so I'm told) sugar, along with just about everything else, was rationed and didn't actually become freely available again until 1953. Our parents had grown up with a considerably reduced sugar diet and limited availability of sweets.

They'd evolved some interesting ways of creating sweets which they passed onto us. One of my favourites was a stick of rhubarb (yes, I did say rhubarb) which was picked out of the garden, given a quick wash and de-stringing and eaten as a sweet. This might seem like an impossibility as rhubarb must be one of the sourest of fruits (actually a vegetable but used like a fruit in cooking) but not when it got the special treatment.

You took a square of greaseproof paper (like tracing paper only for cooking and food storage) and folded it into a cone and twisted the bottom. Then you poured a teaspoon of sugar into the cone and dipped the rhubarb into the sugar and bit the end off. You did this repeatedly until the sugar ran out.

The contrast of the initial sugar burst with the ensuing sourness was a taste sensation but this "treat" was not for the faint hearted especially without the sugar and it was soon passed over in favour of Fruit Salads, Blackjacks, Sherbet Lemons, Spangles, Aniseed Balls, Humbugs, Mint Imperials, Pontefract Cakes, Dolly Mixtures, Gob Stoppers: many straight out of the sweetie jar straight into your hand; four a penny.

The National Health Service continued to offer free dentistry to children. As soon as we had any teeth we were whipped off to the dentist to be checked up. I certainly had a few fillings and an extraction as well. If you were going to have a tooth out your mum was asked, "Cocaine or Gas?"

Cocaine was an injection in your gum to numb it. Gas was a full, knock-out anaesthetic. I had Gas. I can still remember the sight of the approaching mask; the cloying, slightly putrid smell; the hushed tones of the dentist's assistant. And then this bright, sparkling light as consciousness returned with a mouth full of blood to spit into the nearest receptacle.

I don't think we ate huge amounts of sweets or sugar products but we did seem to get a lot of fillings. I have a feeling the dentists must have been paid for the number of fillings they put into our teeth. It seems a bit odd to have fillings in teeth which were going to fall out anyway but they must have had their reasons.

Salad Cream and Tinned Salmon

Sunday Tea was always the same. The best cups and saucers came out of the cupboard along with the starched, white tablecloth and the two-tier cake stand.

Slices of buttered white bread and Hovis; a salad made up of one or two lettuce leaves, a few slices of cucumber and bottled beetroot and two quarters of a tomato; a lump of tinned salmon (preferably John West's) with the bones picked out and the skin removed; half a hard-boiled egg; and a shake of Heinz 57 Varieties salad cream.

For afters: tinned fruit in syrup with Carnation evaporated milk which always curdled if poured over tinned pineapple; fruit scones; sponge cakes; and tea with sugar and a splash of milk.

It was the same if we went to visit our relatives on a Sunday. Whichever aunt, great-aunt, granny or friend of the family we went to see the identical tea was served; only the patterns on the cups and saucers were different.

But the amazing thing is that my husband, who grew up at the other end of the country, had the same Sunday Tea as well. And he says it was exactly the same when they went to visit their relatives too.

The only difference between my family and his was that our cakes were home baked and his came from a baker's shop. And he says they had custard on their tinned fruit.

Did everyone have this meal in the 1950s? Was it replicated from John O'Groats to Land's End? Were there any regional variations? Not much difference between the West Riding of Yorkshire and the East End of London if our experience is anything to go by. And has anyone else, apart from us, continued the tradition?

Tea was always made in a pot. I don't know if teabags had been invented in the 1950s but we always used loose tea and the tea was poured straight from the teapot into the cup without a strainer so there was the danger of swallowing the tea leaves in the dregs if you weren't careful. The pot had to be warmed first with boiling water and the kettle was brought back to boiling point before the tea leaves were scalded. The tea was then left to brew or "mash" as we called it before being poured in a heavy, caffeine laden stream on top of a dash of milk in the bottom of the cup. Usually at least two spoons of sugar were added as well.

My grandad, not Goose Grease Grandad but the other one, worked on the railways. He always took a lemonade bottle filled with cold tea in his "snap bag" along with his sandwiches and whatever else he was having for his lunch. He maintained that not only was it a thoroughly refreshing drink but also, "it did you good." For a man with a lifelong sixty-a-day smoking habit he probably needed more than a few cups of cold tea to do him good.

Grandad was born in 1905 and went to work on the railways as soon as he was able. Getting into the railway wasn't easy and it can only have helped him that his older brother, Arthur, had been working on the railways since grandad was a schoolboy. By 1927, when he got married, grandad had progressed as far as becoming a railway fireman. For those who were employed on the railway a strict hierarchy was enforced to ensure that the drivers of locomotives were the crème de la crème of the industry. Everyone started off as an engine cleaner charged with cleaning all the parts of the huge steam locomotives. Promotion up to "passed cleaner" followed for those who stayed the course which allowed the individual to fire the locomotive in the absence of the regular fireman. This led to becoming a "booked fireman" followed by a "passed fireman" after which, if both oral and practical examinations were passed successfully, the man could become a relief driver and eventually a full driver. The only way to get a promotion was to have served time and to be in the right place at the right time when a vacancy occurred. It could take fifteen years to progress to the top and take charge of one of the mighty steam locomotives but grandad succeeded and we would occasionally see him driving a train on the British Railways line near to where we lived.

Carrier Bags and Nutty Slack

Our street was located between Wakefield city centre and a coal mining village on the outskirts. Wakefield was in the West Riding of Yorkshire. Yorkshire was then divided into three administrative areas called Ridings and the West Riding County Council was the local authority that had responsibility for our school. "W.R.C.C. Now wash your hands" was stamped on every single sheet of every roll of toilet paper in the school's outdoor toilet block. Dark, cob-webby, damp, smelly: you had to be desperate to go in there. The loo-roll was damp too and smelled of disinfectant and it was brittle and hard, like greaseproof paper, and not very effective either.

The Education Department of the W.R.C.C. was headed up by the innovatory Sir Alec Clegg, one of the pioneers of "child-centred" education. For a few weeks our teacher, Mr Phillips, kept disappearing on Wednesday afternoons and then one day he told us to turn the desks back-to-back to make square tables; we started painting murals on a noticeboard in the cloakroom; we made a booklet for a project about a topic of our choice; and we started drawing decorative borders around our handwriting practice. I guess Mr Phillips must have been on one of Sir Alec's training courses at Bretton Hall Teacher Training College.

When we set off for school each morning (that's me and my younger sister and two or three other kids who lived nearby) we turned left from our street onto the pavement at the side of the main road. After several hundred yards we turned left again and walked down a quieter road to the school.

This was what we called the long way round and it was about a mile.

Although the main road wasn't as busy with traffic as it is now it was still dangerous, not least because of the coal lorries that went trundling past firing off scatterings of nutty slack and the odd tennis ball sized lump or worse.

Nutty Slack sounds so charming but it's actually a mix of coal dust and small bits of coal that would be used to keep the fire going if the coal in the coal shed had nearly all been used up.

The Headteacher of the Infants School lived at the bottom of our street. She was known as Miss Wigwam and she was terrifying. She once smacked me on the hand with a ruler because I couldn't do my knitting properly. However, she was a good source of pocket money. She told us that if we collected the lumps of coal from the roadside on the way to and from school she would pay sixpence for a carrier bag full. So, we diligently collected lumps of coal and when the carrier bag was full we plucked up the courage to knock on her door and ask for the money. Naturally, she paid up straight away: she knew she was getting a good bargain.

The carrier bags were made of strong, brown paper with a reinforced gusset at the base. The handles were made from string with small pieces of cardboard strengthening the holes that the string was threaded through. If there was something heavy in the carrier bag the string handles cut into your fingers and hurt. The bags were amazingly resilient and lasted for ages. Unless they got wet and then the bottom of the carrier bag might well sag and split and dump the shopping on the floor.

Once, when we took a bag of coal round to Miss Wigwam she gave us half a crown. She must have read a book about child exploitation.

Next door to us lived Mr Arkenshaw, an elderly widower, a retired miner. He'd lived in the house for years but didn't bother with it much, unlike his garden which was his pride and joy. Especially his rhubarb and dahlias. We enjoyed playing battledore and shuttlecock, a game rather like badminton but with short handled bats. We played it in our garden batting the shuttle back and forth over the washing line but never on a windy day for fear of the shuttle flying over the fence into Mr Arkenshaw's garden. He'd made it clear it wouldn't be returned.

In his spare time Mr Arkenshaw was a coal carver. He had spent months working a massive lump of coal into a scale replica of the Cathedral and he got his picture in the paper. We were invited to go round and admire the model which we did, dutifully. This wasn't his first carving: his sitting room was filled with other jet-like ornaments but the Cathedral was the largest.

Next door to Mr Arkenshaw lived Mr Smithers. His house was surrounded by a dense privet hedge and we were told to keep away from him. No reasons given and we didn't ask. We hardly ever saw him and when we did he had a brown trilby pulled down low on his forehead. Mr Smithers walked along staring down at the floor looking neither left nor right and this, plus the warnings, made us feel uneasy. Even so, his front door became a prime target for door knocking and running away on Mischief Night.

Tricycles and Bicycles

My first bike was actually a tricycle. It was heavy because it was built on a black iron frame with three dustbin lid sized wheels. The wheels had countless shiny spokes which occasionally popped out of their mountings and were bent and difficult to replace. There was a wicker basket on the front of the tricycle. At the rear was a small leather saddle bag and a step for a passenger. Any child who braved the step usually fell off so it wasn't very popular.

My dad had a two-wheeler bike with a cross bar and he would sometimes give us a croggy for a short distance. He cycled to and from work including biking home at dinner time. On Friday afternoons he always came home from work early. He usually brought four vanilla slices from the baker's shop next door to the slaughter house where he worked as a Meat Inspector. He balanced the paper bag of vanilla slices flat on one hand and biked home single handed without dropping or squashing the cakes.

One day he came home from work and told us he'd sold his bike and bought something which was going to change our lives. We hoped it was a car because occasionally he would borrow my mum's auntie's car and take us on an outing for the day. We liked that and looked forward to the infrequent times it happened. My dad learned to drive while he was in the Royal Navy's Fleet Air Arm during the War. When he was de-mobbed he was issued with a driving licence but I don't think he ever passed a driving test. Auntie's car had leather seats and a polished walnut dashboard. It had running boards on the outside and little amber arms that flicked out to indicate if the vehicle was turning left or right. The car was big, old, heavy and a gas-guzzler. Auntie worked for a brewery and she used the car sometimes for beer and soft drinks deliveries. Once when we were out for the day the car's brakes failed as we approached the top of a steep hill. My dad shouted at us to jump out, which we did, and watched in horror as he went hurtling off in the car down the hill. Why he didn't just pull over when he'd managed to slow the car sufficiently for us to jump out, I don't know.

The replacement for dad's bicycle wasn't a car at all. It was a tandem which had been adapted to accommodate two children as well as two adults. Dad was on the front bicycle saddle with me perched in front of him on a child-sized saddle fixed to the cross bar. Mum was on the second bicycle saddle and younger sister had a metal basket seat fixed above the mudguard behind her.

After an adults only trial run on the tandem, dad said it was time for a family outing. Younger sister and I were positioned on the child seats, mum got on in the middle and dad kicked off. It was dreadful and both me and younger sister started screaming. Mum and dad pedalled on while younger sister and me continued screaming at top volume. Soon our hysteria was too much to bear and dad pulled over, lifted us both off our kiddy seats, got back on the tandem and he and mum pedalled off without us. This was much worse and we screamed even louder. Back the parents came and mum walked us home. The tandem was permanently parked down the side of the garden shed and dad walked to work for the next few months.

Books and Comics

I loved the "Bunty" comic and especially "The Four Marys". I couldn't wait for each week's edition to come out so I could get back to St. Elmo's. I really wanted to go to boarding school and consequently devoured Angela Brazil stories and the Chalet School books. Of course, I didn't know anyone who actually went to boarding school. And there was no chance that my parents either wanted to send me or could afford to send me: thank goodness.

My first favourite book was Beatrix Potter's "Peter Rabbit", borrowed from the local public library. We lived within walking distance of the city centre and so had access to a wonderful, dedicated children's library. Housed in Victorian Gothic, the room was large, panelled and echoing. But there were child height chairs where you could sit and look at books while your parents changed their own books. And that's where I fell in love with Pookie.

Pookie: the rabbit with wings; written and illustrated by Ivy Lillian Wallace. I read them all: Pookie and the Gypsies; Pookie's Big Day; Pookie at the Seaside; Pookie Puts the World Right; Pookie in Search of a Home; Pookie believes in Santa Claus.

Pookie might have believed in Santa Claus but I believed in Pookie.

It was only recently that I read Ivy Wallace's amazing story. She was born in Grimsby in 1915. Her parents encouraged Ivy to draw and, recognising her talent, hoped she would become an artist. However, her creative ambitions went in other directions and when she left school she joined Felixstowe repertory theatre as an actress.

On the outbreak of the Second World War she joined the British film industry to help make educational films. She changed direction and began working for the police and it was while working for them that she first thought of Pookie, the winged rabbit.

While working on a police switchboard, she doodled a picture of a fairy sitting on a toadstool with a little rabbit in front. She decided that fairies were too ordinary and erased the fairy and gave wings to the rabbit instead. She christened the rabbit Pookie and wrote a story to go with her illustrations.

In 1946 Ivy turned up, without an appointment, at the offices of publisher William Collins to present her manuscript. As might be expected the response was not encouraging and she returned home disappointed but leaving her manuscript behind.

A few weeks later she was contacted by someone from Collins and asked to attend a meeting at their Glasgow office where the children's book section was based. She met with William Hope Collins who not only accepted the book but fell in love with Ivy as well. William was already estranged from his first wife and a few years later William and Ivy were married, lived happily in Scotland and had two children. Ivy continued to write books for children until William died in 1967 and Collins eventually stopped publishing the books. However, in 1994 Ivy and her daughters re-printed the stories through their own publishing company, Pookie Productions Ltd, although they don't appear to be in print any more.

When I retired some of my colleagues managed to get me a copy of the first Pookie book for a leaving present and I still love it to this day!

Occasionally, my dad would buy me The Children's Newspaper. This was a remarkable publication made to look like a real, but smaller newspaper. Printed in black and white, its stories were selected to be of appeal to children and were from all over the world.

The Children's Newspaper was actually founded by Arthur Mee of Encyclopaedia fame in 1919. He wanted to give children a good grasp of history and geography, world news and science. Apparently, before my time, the popularity of The Childrens' Newspaper began to wane but in the mid-fifties it had a re-launch when items about television and sport were included.

I really enjoyed The Children's Newspaper and always looked forward to getting a copy but I liked "Bunty" better.

When I was learning to read it was Janet and John and Beacon readers at school. However, at home I learned to read with much better easy readers about fairies. The books had bright orangey-red, paper covers and were slim volumes: little more than pamphlets really. There was some writing on the covers in block capitals and the pictures were wonderful. Over the years I asked everyone I knew if they re-called these books; I searched in second hand book shops and charity shops; I looked on the Internet countless times. To no avail. The books stayed as an unreachable memory until, at last, in 2014 I finally tracked them down and just missed a set of twelve on Ebay for £35. I don't actually want to own these books: I just always wanted to know what the books were and to find out why I'd enjoyed them so much.

I discovered on Ebay that the writing in block capitals on the cover of each book was the series title. The series was Simple Reading Steps and the books were written by Eila Mackenzie. The titles in the series were:

Step 1 : Lob-a-Gob
Step 2 : The Rock Fairy and the Sea Fairy
Step 3 : The Tide Fairy
Step 4 : The Cat and the Fairy
Step 5 : The Goblin and His Cap
Step 6 : The Tree Fairy and the Wind Fairy
Step 7 : The Red Fairy
Step 8 : The Pool Fairy and the Rose Fairy
Step 9 : The Wish Fairy
Step 10 : The Goblin Cave
Step 11 : The Rook and the Magpie
Step 12 : The Moon Fairy

The reason I enjoyed the books so much is really simple. In addition to Eila Mackenzie's charming stories, the illustrations were by the renowned children's book artist Margaret Tarrant who specialised in drawings of fairies from the 1920s onwards. I can't find any information about Eila Mackenzie. I loved the books not only for the illustrations but also for the stories so thanks to both ladies for a wonderful start to my reading career.

Classics and Pop

My dad was really keen on classical music and he occasionally got tickets and took us to a Hallé Orchestra concert in Leeds Town Hall. The seats were usually behind the orchestra ideally looking over the timpani player's shoulder. From here you got a good view of the conductor and of the audience facing you in the front row of the stalls.

The building was magnificent: Northern Victorian on the grand scale with marble pillars, plush seats and soaring organ pipes.

The programme was nearly always the same: overture, concerto, interval, symphony, mad-dash for the bus.

We loved going to these concerts especially when the selected music was loud and lively. Before we went we often listened to some of the music on records so when we heard the live performance it had a lovely sense of familiarity.

We often had classical records playing on the gramophone at home. At first they were 78rpm with about 12 discs for a four movement symphony; later they were 33⅓rpm with a symphony on each side.

Once our dad had to go away for a few days to a conference and he said he'd bring back a new record. On his return, after he'd shared out the sticks of seaside rock, he produced a small 45rpm disc in a bright, multi-coloured sleeve. He put it onto the turntable and we were amazed to hear Helen Shapiro belting out "Walking Back to Happiness". This was our first pop record (definitely not the last) and we played it so many times we were word perfect within a day. This record wasn't actually released until 1961 so strictly speaking it's outside the scope of this book. But the moment when my dad acknowledged pop music was a fairly momentous occasion although it was to be a good while before he got his head round the Swinging Sixties.

Practice and Prizes

After grandma died, as well as the grandfather clock, we got the piano. Dad was a really good pianist and although he was sad about the circumstances in which he'd inherited the piano he was delighted to get it.

The piano was a Victorian upright with filled in holes on the front of the case where candlesticks had once been positioned. The piano was dark brown but had lots of wooden in-lay on the front of the casing that lightened it up and you could take off the front and watch the hammers working while you played. It had been in my dad's family for years. During the 1930s when my grandfather temporarily lost his sight and consequently his job the piano had been an impediment to getting any national assistance. The rules were that you sold your carpets, curtains and piano before you could claim any benefits. This was the dreaded Means Test introduced to ensure you were destitute before you got any help.

My grandmother managed to hang on to her things until her husband's sight returned and he was able to go back to work. I suspect she must have had some savings as well which would have been another reason why she didn't qualify for assistance. Her mother had died in 1931 and left a few bob so she'd probably got something under the mattress.

From an early age my dad encouraged me to sit at the piano keyboard and make attempts to play and a few months before my seventh birthday he booked me in for piano lessons with an amazing piano teacher called Miss Heaps.

Miss Heaps always wore a twin-set and a tweed skirt usually in co-ordinated shades of pale blue and mauve. She had a watch on a short strap pinned to the front of her cardigan which looked upside down to me but allowed her to have a good idea of how long the lesson had been going on. She had short, greying hair that curled slightly; she spoke posh Yorkshire; and she was rather intimidating at first. She lived in a beautiful part timber-framed old house near to the city centre. The house still retained a large garden despite the urban re-development that had gone on around it over many decades. As well as mature fruit trees there was space for "the studio". This was where lessons took place and end-of-term concerts for mums and dads and other relatives were performed. There were two upright pianos in the studio and Miss Heaps also had a baby grand piano in the sitting room of her house.

Weekly lessons were booked lasting for half an hour at first and extending to forty five minutes after a few months. Miss Heaps taught the syllabus of the Associated Board of the Royal Schools of Music and her intention was that after one year's study the pupil would be entered for and pass the Grade One examination. This would lead to success every year thereafter in the next grade exams. Failure was not on the menu and this formidable teacher achieved a subsequent 100% pass rate by declining to continue to teach those who did not succeed. Her method was simple: she offered excellent tuition and expected an hour's practice every day at home from each pupil. She had a long waiting list for vacancies in her teaching schedule and once admitted you practiced hard to stay in.

Every year she entered her pupils in the Pontefract and District Music Festival where there were prizes to be won and accolades given. The zenith of my musical career was to win the Under 8's piano competition which resulted in a certificate, a bronze medallion and a photograph in the local newspaper of me and the runner-up.

Miss Heaps charged higher fees than the other piano teachers in the area but she was very generous to her pupils when they passed their exams or did well at the music festival. She had a stock of small plaster busts of classical composers from which she made presentations after each round of exams. By the time I was ten I'd got Handel, Bach and Beethoven and a larger Schubert for gaining distinction in Grade Three. As each old master was acquired he was displayed on top of the piano in our front sitting room where he would keep a watchful eye during piano practice.

When I started piano lessons the piano stool wasn't high enough for me to reach the keyboard. To lift me up, in addition to the seat, my tiny frame was elevated by two volumes of Beethoven's piano sonatas. My feet were nowhere near the pedals either but that didn't matter because Miss Heaps didn't encourage use of the pedals until you were older.

Progress with Miss Heaps was rapid and systematic. This was because she'd discovered a tutorial book that really worked and had her own magic technique: a specially cut and folded piece of paper that sat over the piano keys and reminded the pupil which musical note matched each key. She ended every lesson by playing something by one of the classic composers and then explained why she liked the music or what images the particular piece was meant to evoke. So, along with some piano playing skills which have lasted me all my life, she instilled a love of classical music.

I searched for Miss Heaps on the Ancestry.co.uk Births, Marriages and Deaths records and discovered that she died in 1992 aged 87 years in a residential home for the elderly. So she was in her early fifties when she was my piano teacher. Both my younger sister and I thought she was much older.

Ellen Margaret Heaps was born in 1905 in Wakefield as was her mother, Alice Walsh. Alice married Josiah Heaps in 1904. He originated from Durham but had moved to Wakefield where he was employed as the manager of a draper's shop. Before her marriage Alice lived with her two brothers and two sisters in the same house in

Wakefield where we went for our piano lessons. The brothers were both self-employed joiners and undertakers working from home. The oldest sister was the housekeeper for the family and Alice's other sister, Annie Louise Walsh, was a fully trained school teacher.

After their marriage Alice and Josiah with baby Ellen Margaret moved to Tuxford in Nottinghamshire where Josiah had his own draper's shop. Unfortunately Alice died in 1928 and Josiah and the twenty five year old Ellen Margaret moved back to Wakefield. Then ten years later Ellen Margaret's father died as well and presumably Miss Heaps went to live with her aunts and uncles.

Miss Heaps was always known as Miss E. Margaret Heaps. I think she must have become known as Margaret to avoid confusion between herself and the housekeeper auntie who was also called Ellen.

Once or twice we didn't have our piano lessons in the studio but were invited instead into Miss Heaps' house to play on her baby grand. An old lady sat in the corner of the room to whom we always said, "Good Evening, Miss Walsh" although we didn't know who the old lady was. When I passed my Grade Three piano exam Miss Heaps presented me with a silver medal inscribed on the back: "The Louise Walsh Musicianship Award". The old lady in the corner must have been the school teacher aunt, Annie Louise Walsh.

Miss Heaps continued to live with Aunt Louise in the family home until 1962 when they moved to another house in a neighbouring street. Miss Walsh died in 1965 and Miss Heaps lived on for another twenty years in their new home. It made me quite sad to work all this out and I hope this very special lady didn't die alone in her old people's home.

Radio and Television

Like just about everyone else we had a radio that was encased in a large wooden box with a few dials on the front and a circle of fine lattice-work mesh over the speaker. The dials were to tune the radio and the station choices were BBC, BBC and BBC: The Light Programme, The Home Service and the Third Programme.

In the afternoon we had "Listen with Mother" with Daphne Oxenford and the never to be forgotten "Are you sitting comfortably? Then I'll begin". We listened to "Children's Hour" at tea-time featuring Larry the Lamb and Toytown. And then "The News". On Sunday it was "Two Way Family Favourites" with record requests between people at home and their relatives abroad in the British Army. BFPO40 seemed a very popular address. "Mrs Dale's Diary" and "Woman's Hour" were our mother's favourites although our dad preferred the Third Programme which was more highbrow.

The radio was known as "The Wireless" even though you had to plug the wires into the electric socket in the wall. Quite often it crackled with interference and you had to turn it off. If you tuned the dials away from the BBC sometimes you got a voice in an unknown language but usually it was just a high pitched wail.

Our uncle worked for a big electrical shop and he knew all about televisions. One day he delivered a television to our house. It had an even bigger wooden cabinet than the wireless and a very small screen. Of course, the picture was black and white. Now we had "Watch with Mother" which included "Picture Box"; "Rag, Tag and Bobtail"; "Andy Pandy"; "Bill and Ben the Flowerpot Men" and "The Woodentops".

We always watched "Dixon of Dock Green":

"Evening all."

"The Lone Ranger":

"Hi-Yo Silver!"

and

"Robin Hood! Robin Hood! Riding through the glen!"

There are loads of clips on YouTube if you want to waste an hour or two as I did!

Although not strictly in the nineteen fifties, Princess Margaret's wedding to the society photographer Anthony Armstrong Jones was the biggest television event we'd seen. It was the first royal wedding to be broadcast and was watched by an audience of over twenty million viewers. The build-up was considerable because in the 50s the princess had fallen in love with a divorced man who worked for the royal family. Divorce was a taboo subject as far as the royals were concerned in those days and Princess Margaret capitulated and gave up on the love of her life. She met Tony in 1958; was engaged to him in 1959 and they were married in 1960. We were given the day off school to celebrate the marriage and watch it on the television but we got fed up after a while and went out to play.

Nits and Sniffs

We had our hair washed every Friday night with Vosene shampoo. This smelled of antiseptic and mothballs and if it got in your eyes it killed.

The rinsing water had a tablespoon of vinegar stirred into it so by the time hair washing night was over our heads smelled very odd.

Of course, I didn't realise at the time that the vinegar was a part of our mother's war on nits; similarly the ritual combing while your hair was drying out. The combing was done with one of those fine tooth combs which dragged through the tangles - we called them "lugs" - and pulled your hair out by the roots.

I don't remember ever actually having head lice as a child but there was a girl in our class at school who did.

The teacher made her sit by herself.

We had those wooden desks with a lift-up lid, a storage space underneath, an inkwell and a channel to keep your pen and pencil in. The desks were joined together in twos and everyone in the class was allocated a partner whom you were forced to sit in close proximity to all day and every day.

Except for Alice who had nits.

There were forty three children in the class and the twin desks were arranged in three rows down the length of the room. The teacher sat at the head of the class barricaded behind a big wooden desk which screened the open, coal fire - the only source of heating in winter - from the rest of the room.

Most of the time the children in the class were very quiet and extremely well behaved. This wasn't because we were inspired by the lessons or motivated by our charismatic teacher. To the contrary! But there was a good reason for our compliance and passivity. "Miss" had made it very clear at the start of the term that anyone who mis-behaved would be made to sit next to Alice. And no-body wanted that.

In the playground everyone mucked in together and Alice joined in and charged around with the rest of the class. However once we were all back in the classroom she was segregated, humiliated and demonised in that really dreadful manner.

The twin desks were so small and closely packed that coughs, sneezes and assorted other diseases passed round the class at top speed: Measles; German Measles; Scarlet Fever; Chicken Pox; Mumps; Flu; Tonsillitis. Polio and Diphtheria were still a threat and once a Smallpox scare resulted in mass, urgent, immunisation.

"Don't forget your hankie!" was one of several daily exhortations made both at home and school in an attempt to stop the spread of winter ailments. Though how carrying around a square of snot encrusted cotton all day was good for your health I can't imagine.

Any child with a bad cold who'd forgotten their handkerchief would sit and sniff until eventually "Miss" bawled out:

"If you've not got a handkerchief, use your sleeve!"

Sewing and Knitting

At school in the 1950s girls learned to sew and knit. I don't know what the boys did but it wasn't sewing and knitting.

I hated knitting and I couldn't do it because I was left-handed and we were shown what to do by a right-handed teacher and it didn't make much sense.

It started when we were in the top class of the Infants school and we had to knit a dish-cloth out of special woven cotton called dish-cloth string. It was white; about as thick as spaghetti and came into the classroom in large skeins.

The first task was to wind off the required amount. We worked in pairs: one girl holding the skein stretched out across both hands while the other one rolled herself a ball of dish cloth string and then we swapped over.

The knitting needles were made out of wood and were thick. We called them "pokers" because they were about the same size as the poker used for the coal fires in our homes. A loop was tied in the string and then as the teacher demonstrated we tried to form the first row of stitches. Some girls managed to do it and many, like me, did not. So the teacher came round and quickly "cast on" our stitches for us.

The following week, out came the knitting needles with their single row of stitches and your name on a piece of paper skewered through one of the needles.

Once again, teacher demonstrated and we tried to copy and a few succeeded. Then a few more got the hang of it and the teacher came round and did the first row of knitting for the rest of the class. Time to stop, stab the work again with your name tag and put it away until next time.

This was repeated week by week with gradually more pupils working out what to do and the teacher doing a couple more lines of knitting for the dwindling group who couldn't manage it. By now the dishcloths were a couple of inches long and as each week passed, inch by inch, they grew until all members of the class were being left to complete their dish-cloths for themselves.

Eventually they were finished: no longer pristine, rather a grubby grey and not completely without a few decorative loops, lumps and holes. The dish-cloth took about half the year to make and we had to pay one shilling to be allowed to take it home for our mothers. "The best dishcloth I ever had" was the white lie told me by my mum when I presented it to her.

For the other half of the year we had sewing class. We were given a square of fabric with regular small holes in it; a cocktail-stick-thick needle with a blunt end; and some soft embroidery cottons in bright colours.

From the edge of the fabric we had to count in three holes and then sew in and out of the same two holes over and over three times to make an anchor for the thread. Then we would go in and out of the holes round the perimeter of the fabric until we got back to the start.

After choosing a contrasting colour which was anchored in the same way, and on the same side as the original knot, we set off again round the edge, threading the new colour in and out of the first round of stitches. This was repeated on the next series of holes inside the two-tone border; and then again and again until at last the centre of the fabric was reached.

Finally the surplus fabric outside the first row of stitches was carefully fringed by pulling off the horizontal threads and the "table mat" was complete. After payment of the obligatory shilling it could go home to grace the sideboard, dressing table or any other flat surface which would benefit from being covered.

The following September we left the Infant school and went across the playground to the neighbouring Junior school and our stitching education continued: still for girls only, of course. I never found out what the boys did at that time every week.

Pen and Ink

At school we learnt to write with thick stubby pencils before transferring to thinner pencils at the end of Infants school. Halfway through the Juniors we were introduced to pen and ink.

In the lower Juniors we were taught to write "joined-up" by the simple expedient of copying out "The Lord's Prayer" every Monday morning into our handwriting exercise books. Moving onto pen and ink was highly anticipated: one of life's milestones.

The pen was a thin wooden stick with a metal holder on one end into which was inserted a metal nib. This was dipped into an inkwell located in the top right corner of the desk. We had to work out how to load the nib with sufficient ink to write without dripping ink over the desk and the exercise book. No mean feat when you're only about nine years old. Once that hurdle was overcome the next step was to learn how to write without splattering the page or making smudges.

As a left handed person it was almost impossible to write without smudging because the left-right orientation of English means that the left hander has no option but to drag their hand over the wet writing unless an alternative technique was evolved. Mine was to push forward into the paper although some left handers twist their hand round and write over the top of the line.

My early efforts at joined up writing in ink were fairly disastrous despite my best efforts but salvation was at hand. In the next class our enlightened teacher allowed us to bring from home a fountain pen if we had one. For Christmas I received an Osmiroid fountain pen with a dark blue marbled effect barrel. It also had a special nib designed for left-handers which made writing with ink a lot easier.

Whether you used a fountain pen or a dip-in pen you were issued, in case of drips or splashes, with a postage stamp size square of blotting paper. The blotting paper was usually pink but occasionally green and was meant to last for a whole half term. I've often read in school story books about pupils putting scrunched up bits of blotting paper into the inkwell and then firing the ink soaked pellet across the classroom at some unsuspecting target but I can honestly say no-one at my school ever dared to do anything like that.

Dolls and Houses

My first doll was a Rosebud. I didn't give her a name because the word Rosebud was moulded into her back. She was made from some form of hard, creamy coloured plastic which we called 'pot'. Rosebud had limbs jointed with rubber bands and occasionally one would come off. It was a real struggle to get it hooked back on. Rosebud's hair was moulded onto her head in curls and she had blue, staring eyes with lids that flicked up and down.

My younger sister had a Rosebud doll too which was the same as mine except it was black with orange eyes. This was a bit of a surprise as we had never met anyone who was black. Her Rosebud also had a voice box in the back underneath the moulded Rosebud name-tag. When tilted my sister's Rosebud would make a plaintive sound of "mama, mama" which was rather eerie. My younger sister has kept her Rosebud doll for well over fifty years but the rubber has perished and the head and arms have fallen off. Fortunately the voice box no longer functions. As well as making clothes for us children, our mum made outfits for the dolls and black Rosebud still wears to this day the clothes our mum made for her.

After the "pot" dolls we had vinyl dolls. These were made out of a softer plastic and had "real hair" which was rooted through pin-holes in the doll's head. The hair was long enough to wash, comb and style. The arms and legs moved and didn't fall off. One of them was named Josephine but I'm not sure if this was mine or my younger sister's. One day my younger sister scribbled all over my Josephine with biro which wouldn't wash off.

One year we spent all our Christmas and Birthday money on clothes for our Faerie Glen dolls. These were smaller dolls than the others for which you could buy various outfits. A pre-cursor of Sindy and Barbie, I suppose. I bought my Faerie Glen doll a red, plastic mac and a pair of wellies which cost 7/6: a truly extortionate price but at the time I thought it was money well spent. I wish I'd kept the doll and the outfits because looking on Ebay the 1950s Faerie Glen dolls and clothes seem to be very rare and worth a lot more now than we paid for them then.

My last doll was a "teenager" doll. She was made out of vinyl and had long, peroxide blonde, hair which was pulled up into a high pony-tail. She was jointed at the waist so she could turn from side to side. She had disproportionately long legs and feet permanently elevated for her high-heeled shoes. And she had pointy boobs. She came with cami-knickers; a sticking out skirt; a blouse which tied at the front under her boobs; and a pair of white stilettos. Such style!

I had a doll's house as well which had two rooms upstairs and two rooms downstairs; a staircase and bathroom in the middle and a hinged front that opened out so you could play with it. The walls were red brick and the roof tiles were green. It had electric lights in all the rooms and a battery pack in the roof to power them. It was occupied by a family of four: mum, dad and two kids (a boy and a girl) and it was fully carpeted, curtained and furnished. I only found out years later that my uncle had made the house from a kit and my mum had done the fitting out. The furniture came from the Doll's House Furniture Shop in Leeds. The shop was down an arcade and the window was filled with miniature room settings. There was a Doll's Hospital next door which my teddy bear had to go to once to get his eye sewn back in.

Escalators and Menageries

Most of our everyday food was bought locally or delivered by the milkman, bread man, fruit man, fish man or butcher's van. Once every couple of months we went shopping in Leeds and the highlight was going round Lewis's which was a huge department store located in The Headrow, the city's main thoroughfare. Lewis's wasn't the same as the present day John Lewis shops; this was a completely different chain of department stores. The first store was opened in Liverpool in 1856 by an entrepreneur named David Lewis. Lewis was a Londoner with a Jewish background and a business in men's tailoring. He opened the store to sell the clothes he manufactured and the business expanded rapidly into women's clothing and other goods. The store was successful and Lewis opened another store in Manchester in 1877 and another in Birmingham in 1885. Lewis sold out to a different company who expanded the business further opening stores in Glasgow, Stoke-on-Trent and Leicester as well as Leeds. In 1951 the company actually bought Selfridges in London and continued to maintain a strong retail position until 1991 when it went into administration. David Lewis, the founder of Lewis's, died in 1885 and left thousands of pounds to various charities in Liverpool.

The Leeds store was opened in September 1932 and was a great success. The architect was G. W. Atkinson who visited America to look at department store design before starting on the Leeds branch of Lewis's. No expense was spared to create for the first time in Leeds a lavish and exciting shopping experience. The floors and walls of the new store were covered in marble and the escalator was the first to be installed in Leeds. One hundred thousand people visited Lewis's on opening day and there were so many departments "Ask Me" girls were employed to help customers find what they were looking for.

The wonderful escalator in Lewis's had shiny wooden hand rails and steps made of strips of polished wood which miraculously disappeared at the top just before you jumped off. At Christmas you went right to the top of the store to Santa's Grotto where the real Santa was waiting to hear your Christmas wishes and gave you a little present to be going on with. I didn't realise your parent paid for you to have this treat and I never saw any money change hands. Until it was your turn to see Santa, you waited in a queue looking at festive scenes of elves and things you might like to possess which conveniently were available elsewhere in the store. Then each child went into the grotto alone, sat on Santa's knee and told him what they were hoping to get for Christmas. His answer was the same every year: "I'll see what I can do. And you be a good girl. Off you go, Happy Christmas, Ho, Ho, Ho."

Before leaving the store we always went down on the escalator to the basement to visit the menagerie. This was where customers could buy pets and there were usually some puppies, kittens, rabbits and tortoises available. There was a tank with a snake in it and a cage that housed a couple of monkeys. They were only tiny monkeys but they were lively. We would stand and watch them jumping around and climbing on the bars at the front of the cage for as long as we were allowed to stay there.

Once, my younger sister got too close to the cage. She was wearing a hat, one of the felt, cloche style with turned up brim that were popular for girls to wear with their best coats then. To stop the hat blowing off in the wind there was a piece of elastic which fitted under her chin and kept the hat in place. On this occasion the monkey reached through the bars of the cage, grabbed the hat and tried to pull it in. A tussle ensued between my dad and the monkey with younger sister's head in the middle until the hat was retrieved and we left the basement in a flurry of tears and laughter.

The hat grab incident didn't put us off visiting the monkeys but a subsequent incident did. On one of our shopping trips to Leeds our grandmother came with us but we still made the basement visit at the end of the day. We were standing watching the monkeys as usual when one of them climbed up the bars, turned full frontal and wee'd straight at grandma. Fortunately, she was agile too and she managed to jump back out of range with only a few splashes on her coat to evidence the attack. After that we didn't visit the monkeys again. I hope the management eventually had the good sense to send the monkeys to a zoo and close down the pets department.

Steam Trains and Pennies

At the top of our street was a gate going into some allotments. If you kept to the path straight ahead you were allowed to cross the allotments without being yelled at by one of the old boys leaning on a fork or shovel.

At the end of the path was a "kissing gate" and then you were out onto the lane which lead down to the railway track. You went only a few yards before coming to the security fence which protected the track. It wasn't a crossing point: the lane just stopped there.

The fence was robust and higher than any of us kids but we could climb up two bars and then rest our arms and chins on the top bar.

And wait for the trains.

They were usually goods trains; mainly transporting coal which we could see piled up high in each of the trucks: black loaf sized lumps; massed little stones; great, gleaming boulders. Sometimes the cargo was in sealed tanks: we didn't know what they contained and the numbers and letters on the side of each tank gave no clues. Occasionally there was a passenger train; probably there was a diversion on another section of the line, I suppose. Then we would wave and the passengers often waved back and if they didn't we stuck our tongues out and occasionally they did that back too.

Because the trains travelled slowly you could see the engine driver and the fireman inside the locomotive cabin. They always waved and called out but the train was so noisy we didn't hear what they said but we called back anyway; usually "chuck us a penny, Mister" and sometimes they did.

It was more likely to be a handful of ha'pennies which would fly over our heads and we'd leap off the fence and start scrabbling in the gravel to grab what we could.

The coinage was so different: half-pennies; pennies; threepenny bits; sixpences; shillings; florins; half-crowns and paper notes for ten shillings and pound notes. There were notes in larger denominations but I didn't see one until I was much older.

We had farthings as well but I don't re-call ever spending them. They had an imprint of a little bird, a wren I think, on one side and the King's head on the other. That would be George VI; I don't remember ever seeing Queen Elizabeth II on a farthing. They were worth a quarter of one penny and even in those days you couldn't buy much for that. My favourite coin was a threepenny bit or 'thrupence' as it was known. It was twelve-sided and had the queen's head on one side and a portcullis on the other; it was a lovely yellowy-golden colour with a hint of green. I used to think they were doubloons that had come off a pirate's ship.

You only needed to save up four threepenny bits to have the equivalent of one shilling and eight threepenny bits equalled a florin. A florin was worth two shillings. We didn't call it a florin very often: it was a 'two bob bit' by which you can work out that one shilling was a 'bob'. Half a crown was two shillings and sixpence or 'two and six' but I can't remember ever seeing a whole crown other than as a commemorative coin.

I once got a ten bob note for a birthday present and I thought I was rich. It would be the equivalent of about £10 today so I suppose, from a child's point of view, I was.

Seaside and Holidays

Each year in the summer we had a week's holiday at the seaside. One year we stayed at Mrs Jagger's in Blackpool where we made sandcastles on the beach and went to the circus in the Blackpool Tower. A couple of times we stayed at a guest house called "Lyndhurst" in Scarborough that I vividly remember had a green front door. In Scarborough we went looking for crabs in the rock pools left behind when the tide went out and had donkey rides on the sand before our last night treat at the penny arcades.

Other years we stayed in a chalet but not a chalet of the picturesque, carved wooden eaved, mountainside, snow-clad variety of the Swiss Alps. These were more like asbestos garages positioned in uniform rows on bleak fields at the edge of a town between the sea and the countryside.

One was in Mablethorpe which is somewhere on the Lincolnshire coast near Skegness. The chalet was newly built and the roads around the holiday park were still under construction. It was unfortunate that it rained every day because having travelled there by train and bus we had no transport. There was nowhere else to go except the beach which was fine when the rain stopped: only it didn't. There was nowhere to dry the clothes and only a small two bar electric fire which was fuelled by shillings which went into a box on the wall and were burnt out in seconds. We arrived on Saturday and were supposed to stay for a week but by Thursday enough was enough and the suitcase full of damp washing was packed up and we caught the first bus out on Friday morning.

Another year we stayed in a well-established chalet park near Bridlington on the Yorkshire coast. We travelled to Bridlington by train and then after a short bus ride arrived at the camp site tucked into the cliffs behind Thornwick Bay. The chalet was borrowed from the auntie of my mum's friend although it still had to be paid for. It had been in their family for some years and had an idiosyncratic charm based on peeling paint, blurred windows, cracked plant pots and an outdoor, chemical toilet. The kitchen had been well used and was unfamiliar with Brillo pads or scouring powder and my mum spent the first evening of her holiday scrubbing the floor, bleaching the sink and de-crusting the cooker. At first we refused completely to go in the outside toilet which was a corrugated iron chamber behind the chalet with a front door opening and a Perspex roof to let in a little light. The Perspex was layered with guano and the light that managed to get through was minimal. The box enclosed a large metal bucket called Elsan containing a liquid chemical disinfectant and the bodily functions of the previous occupants. There was a toilet seat fixed to the top of the bucket and every few days a lorry toured the site emptying the Elsans and taking away their contents for disposal. After considerable maternal coaxing we braved Elsan wearing one of dad's large cotton handkerchiefs as a triangular mask.

Naturally it rained for at least part of every day, creating the climatic conditions on which the indigenous population of ear-wigs thrived. The chalet was constructed from wooden panels impregnated with Creosote and the ear-wigs inhabited the cracks between the slats when they weren't causing terror to small girls as they crawled over pillows, blankets and window sills.

The beach was down a long, steep hill with steps in some places and rough scrambling in the rest. There was a bit of sand and a lot of pebbles, smooth white chalk pebbles ranging from marble to boulder sizes. It was idyllic and despite the rain we had a lovely time there. Caves and rock pools; foam topped waves that came in fast when the tide turned; crabs, starfish, razor shells and sea urchins; every variety of seabird caterwauling on the cliffs. The week passed quickly and despite the accommodation my younger sister and I enjoyed the holiday but my mum said she wouldn't go back there again not even if someone paid her, and she didn't.

One summer our family suddenly became very rich. My dad bought a car: a green, second-hand Ford Consul with fake leopard skin seat covers. We went on holiday for two weeks instead of the usual seven days. And, not only was the holiday for two weeks but it wasn't Blackpool, Scarborough or Brid!

We went to London and then to Littlehampton which is in Sussex on the south coast of England.

Even though we'd got the car we still went on the train to London where we stayed for three nights in a B&B in South Kensington. We did all the sights and had a day at London Zoo. While we were in the zoo there was a terrible storm and everyone rushed to get inside out of the rain. We managed to cram into the Reptile House and stayed squashed in there while the thunder and lightning played itself out. Later we saw the famous Chimps Tea Party where four chimpanzees were taken by their keepers to sit at a picnic table and drink tea and eat sandwiches, cakes and lollipops. The highlight, of course, was when one of the chimps drank straight out of the teapot. The chimps didn't seem to mind being the source of so much public amusement and at least they weren't wearing dresses which was what happened when you saw chimps at the circus.

We went to look at Buckingham Palace and the Houses of Parliament which we recognised from the H.P. Sauce bottle. I wondered what brown sauce had in common with the Houses of Parliament. Apparently the recipe was devised in 1895 by a Nottingham grocer called Frederick Garton. He adopted the name H.P. for his sauce when he found out that it was being served in the Houses of Parliament. In 1905 Garton sold his recipe to the Midland Vinegar Company who marketed it widely. Although the company which owns the brand has changed several times and it is now manufactured in the Netherlands, H.P. Sauce remains the most popular British brown sauce to this day.

We went to see the Tower of London and threw pennies to the mudlarks at the foot of Tower Bridge; admired lots of paintings in the National Gallery; fed the ducks in St. James' Park and the pigeons in Trafalgar Square. We also paid our respects to the Unknown Soldier in Westminster Abbey.

Then we travelled on another train down to Littlehampton where we stayed in a caravan in a holiday camp near the sea. The suitcases had been sent on in advance and miraculously they were waiting for us in the camp-site office. That summer was one of the hottest on record and we spent the week on the beach turning rapidly from bright pink to light tan along with countless other families doing the same.

We spent a couple of days with a family who lived near the New Forest. My dad had been friendly with them when he was younger but hadn't seen them for several years. We went to Portsmouth and having met Nelson on his column back in London were amazed at how small his Victory ship was in real life. Finally we took the train back to Yorkshire and after that the money was spent and things went back to normal except we still had the car.

I didn't find out the reason for this sudden burst of affluence until years later. It turned out that my parents had locked themselves into a life insurance package that was proving a big drain on the family resources so they'd decided to cut their losses, cash in the policy and have a splurge.

And I'm glad they did. We had a great time on the holiday and having a car of our own was transformational. Pity about the leopard skin seats though which caused static if you didn't sit still.

Bonfires and Fireworks

Apart from a few pennies each week for pocket money and Christmas and Birthday gifts, we didn't have much actual cash to spend. One of our best sources of income came at the end of the year and was directed towards a specific purpose.

On November 5th it was Bonfire Night. The preceding weeks were spent in a frenzy of collecting wood and anything else which would burn ready for the communal bonfire which was held on the neighbouring allotments. This "chubbing" was not always a friendly affair if there was more than one bonfire being built in the neighbourhood. Often as much time could be spent guarding the growing pile of wood from raiding parties as was spent collecting additional stuff to burn.

At the same time plans were underway for "Penny for the Guy". A Guy Fawkes was made out of an old coat stuffed with newspaper with some sort of a ball for the head decorated with joke specs and crowned with an old cap. Fixing the head to the body was a challenge and stuffed trouser legs were an optional extra as Guy would sit in a pram or pushchair and be wheeled round the street door to door.

Knock, knock.

"Penny for the Guy, please."

"Sod off!"

"You were here last night."

"Sweep the path and I'll think about it."

"Do me an errand to the shop and I'll give you a penny."

"All right, this time, but no more."

By persistence and cheek we gradually accumulated a few shillings which was all spent on fireworks to add to the display on the big night on the allotments. At the appointed hour Guy was ceremoniously positioned on the top of the pyre and somebody's dad (not mine) did a judicious sprinkling of petrol to get the usually sodden pile of rubbish alight. The fireworks were all set off and a few naughty boys threw a handful of bangers around until they got a good telling off. Cups of tea were brought out from the nearest house and pieces of home-made, ginger cake called Yorkshire Parkin were passed round. Usually that was the extent of the refreshments but one year someone organised a Pie and Pea Supper. The next morning we collected up the remains of the fireworks and kept them for a while until they were old and soggy and they were thrown in the bin.

The few shillings we made were a stark contrast to my husband's "Penny for the Guy" income. He approached the task on an industrial scale with a Guy of which Madame Tussaud's would have been proud and a pitch at the bus-stop outside his front door. This was on the main bus route taking commuters home into the East End at the end of the day and from the moment school finished he was at that bus-stop meeting and greeting another bus every minute or two. The pitch was so lucrative it was viciously fought over but usually the justice of the street prevailed and the proximity of his front door to the bus-stop gave him an inbuilt advantage in the form of his formidable grandmother if the fighting got too rough.

Sundays and Sunday School

Most Sundays we went to church twice: once in the morning to the Sunday service and again in the afternoon to Sunday School. In the church on Sunday mornings we always sat in the same place; so did everyone else. We sat behind a man who had a special seat with a tall stick on the end of the pew. He always had his hand in his pocket jingling his change and at collection time he went round with a wooden plate lined with red velvet for everyone to put their donations in. I never saw him put any money in the plate himself though and the jingling didn't sound any different after he'd taken the collection than it did before.

After the service we walked home and had our Sunday dinner: roast meat, roast potatoes, vegetables and gravy. Goose Grease Grandad always came to visit us on Sundays, arriving just in time for dinner, leaving straight after tea and having a snooze in between. He needed the snooze because he got off the bus a few stops away from our house and had a Sunday lunch time drink or two in the nearest pub.

Every few weeks we would go and see him in his prefab for our mum to do the cleaning for him. She told him to take me and my younger sister for a walk so she could get on. We went for walks with grandad in the countryside around the mining village where he'd lived since 1897. As we walked he told us stories about his life as a pit pony boy. He'd started working in the pit when he was twelve years old. The highlight of our walk was when we passed a field where he said the ponies had spent their summer holidays; apparently they got two weeks above ground and presumably that was enough to keep them going for the rest of the year. We always used to stop there and eat a bag of butterscotch sweets.

As he got older grandad progressed from pit pony boy to being an underground worker. His job wasn't to hew the coal; he was in maintenance and his job was to make sure the cables which pulled the machinery were safe. Later he became responsible for the overground cables and one day he noticed there was a serious flaw in one of the cables he was working on. This was reported to the company and a terrible disaster was averted. As a reward for his vigilance the grateful management awarded him a bottle of wine every year at Christmas. For a man who enjoyed a pint of Guiness (or several) a few times a week this must have seemed a poor reward.

After eating our Sunday pudding and helping mum with the pots we left grandad snoozing and walked back to church for the afternoon session.

Sunday School was held in the church hall next door to the church. It was an ugly, red-brick construction thrown up, like the church and so many of the surrounding houses, in the 1920s. At Sunday School we were divided into classes just like everyday school and we had a lesson each week about a different aspect of the life and times of Jesus. At the end of every lesson you were given a special stamp that had a picture of that week's story on it to stick into a little booklet which was supposed to remind you of what you'd learned that week and in previous weeks. The booklet was also your passport to treats. At the end of the year if you had enough stamps in your booklet you could go to the Sunday School Christmas Party and you were eligible to go on the next year's Sunday School outing to the seaside.

The Sunday School Christmas Party was a big event held on the Sunday next before Christmas at which you could wear your new winter dress made specially for the festive season which you had to keep clean and not spill anything on or else. Games were played with lots of charging about the hall while one of the Sunday School teachers bashed away on the piano with countless variants of "and when the music stops..." After the games refreshments were eaten at long trestle tables covered in sheets of white fish and chip shop paper placed strategically around the sides of the room. Everyone brought their own plate and cup from home and at Christmas Party tea time the Sunday School teachers and a few of the mums went round with plates of sandwiches: fish paste, meat paste or jam; biscuits: jammy dodgers, custard creams, chocolate bourbons; and to finish off, a Wagon Wheel. Increasingly watery orange squash was poured into the cups and usually onto the chip paper too. When the party tea was all eaten it was time to go home and everyone got a goodie bag with a few sweets in it and exhortations to "don't eat them all at once, save some for next year."

There was one guest who was conspicuous by his absence at our Christmas party. We knew he didn't live on earth but we'd heard so much about him in the preceding weeks; we knew he would know if we weren't "good little girls and boys"; we'd prayed to him every night that our dearest wish for Christmas would come true. But Santa Claus was never invited to the Christmas party. Not because he and his elves were too busy getting ready for Christmas but because the Anglican church we attended did not subscribe to the myth of jolly old St. Nick.

For the Sunday School Summer Outing we travelled on a specially hired bus all the way to Bridlington but we took our own meat paste, fish paste or jam sandwiches. The first hour or so after we arrived was spent clambering down the sand dunes, digging and paddling and charging around. But after we'd eaten our gritty lunches the Sunday School teachers marked out a large section of the beach for organised games like rounders and French cricket. There was lots of standing around waiting for a turn to bat and much shouting, cheering and surreptitious jeering at any nearby Sunday Schools from other places. By half past three we were back on the bus and on our way home gustily singing choruses of Ten Green Bottles and One Man Went to Mow.

Leopard Skin and Geiger Counters

In World War Two my dad was in the Fleet Air Arm and for part of his service he was stationed near Freetown in Sierra Leone, West Africa. He didn't talk about this part of his life very often but he had a few souvenirs which he would occasionally get out and show us.

He had a small carved wooden elephant with tiny ivory tusks and a gold jewellery box that he'd brought back from Africa as presents for his mother. After his mother died he'd got the gifts back and given them to our mum. The jewellery box had a pale blue velvet lining and was carved with tiny figures and tropical scenery. We thought it was solid gold and worth a fortune but it was really only tin with some gold lacquer on it.

He'd somehow managed to bring home with him from Africa a ceremonial dagger in a leopard skin case and a matching shield. The knife was about two feet long and four inches wide at the widest part. It was quite thick and not very sharp so he let us play sword fights with it. The shield was about the size of a dustbin lid and had a wooden frame with leopard skin stretched over it. We knew Tarzan quite well so this provided the context for our imaginations.

My dad kept these treasures in the loft along with the Royal Navy folding bed he'd brought home at the end of the War. This was a complicated wooden structure with folding criss-cross legs which supported a length of hessian. Onto this was placed his Navy mattress roll and then the bed clothes. We used it as a guest bed on the rare occasions when anyone came to stay over.

In the garden shed was the best wartime souvenir of all. We called it the Geiger counter. It was a box painted in naval grey which, when opened up, had dials, switches and a small glass cover over a swinging needle, a bit like a miniature speedometer. The dials were numbered and if twisted they rotated back on themselves making a loud clicking noise as they turned. The Geiger counter was kept with some more conventional tools like screwdrivers and spanners in a folded up roll of cloth. I suspect all these thing were part of my dad's maintenance equipment when he worked as a radio and radar mechanic in the Fleet Air Arm.

We loved playing with the Geiger counter. The garden shed only had a small window and was dark inside when the door was closed: ideal for being in a submarine with the Geiger counter making sure we didn't get lost. On other days the shed was a rocket headed for the moon with the Geiger counter playing its part in getting us there. And when we were playing our more usual games of dolls, tea parties, hospitals, schools and shopping the Geiger counter could be relied on to tick away the time or just be a good weight to stop things blowing away.

When we moved house in 1962 the Geiger counter and the leopard skin sword and shield all went out for the dustbin men. I've still got the elephant and the jewellery box though in my family history store.

You can find out more about my dad's wartime experiences in another book I've published. It's title is Think I Prefer the Tinned Variety: The Diary of a Petty Officer in the Fleet Air Arm during World War II. The book starts off explaining that my father, Norman Buckle, was nineteen years old when in 1943 he arrived in West Africa as a wartime volunteer in the Fleet Air Arm of the Royal Navy. He came from a coal mining village in South Yorkshire and he'd never been abroad before. Norman kept a personal diary during his naval service which documents some of his experiences, thoughts and emotions. He died in 1978 aged fifty four years and his war time diary remained stored in an old suitcase in several lofts and attics for over thirty years.

After I retired I spent many a happy hour researching both my own and my husband's family histories. Eventually though, I came to a dead end after I'd explored every aspect of the lives of even the most distant relatives. I'd already sorted through a box of old photos that had been in the loft for years and had labelled as many of them as I could. Now I turned my attention to an old, homemade, hard backed notebook with the initials N.B. stencilled on the deteriorating hessian cover. I knew this was a collection of photographs and postcards that my dad had stuck in the book accompanied by captions in his tiny, precise handwriting. Folded into the book were lots of pages torn from an old diary for 1944 and several sheets of notepaper covered in that same spidery handwriting.

I'd read all of this many years previously and knew that it recorded his time at a Royal Navy airbase known as His Majesty's Ship (H.M.S.) Spurwing in Hastings, near Freetown, Sierra Leone, West Africa. It also covered the weeks he'd spent in Australia prior to being sent to Ponam in the Admiralty Islands (part of present day Papua New Guinea). I read the diary again and was intrigued by what my dad had written. As I deciphered his handwriting a number of questions were raised in my mind. I decided to type up the manuscript to make the extracts more legible and accessible and then passed copies to my two sisters. Like me, they were intrigued and also prompted to ask questions in relation to what they were reading. When he was alive, our dad had never really spoken about his war time experiences and when we were younger we hadn't been interested in what he'd been doing thirty years previously. Now we had the interest we didn't have the person with the answers.

I decided to use the skills I'd acquired in pursuing our family histories to track down more of the background to our dad's war. The more I read and the more of the background I understood, the more interested I became. I paid for a copy of dad's records from the Royal Navy Archives but these gave incomplete details of his service. Then my sister discovered in her loft, in another old suitcase, a folder containing the original documents that were Norman's Fleet Air Arm records: they detailed in chronological order where he'd been and what his role was. There were other documents that added further to our dad's story.

I researched more of the background to the diary to try and understand Norman's story better. Eventually the annotated diary was published as an ebook in October 2012 seventy years to the day since my dad signed up for his war service.

And finally

Thank you for reading Cabbage and Semolina. I hope you've enjoyed reading my memories whether you're of the same generation as me or older or younger. And I hope I've inspired you to record and share some of your own memories too. Don't leave it too late; you never know what's round the corner.

I also want to thank my younger sister, Helen, and my husband, Michael, for sharing with me some of their memories of their 1950s childhoods and for encouraging me to publish this book.

I hope you'll want to read some more of our books.
They're all available from the Amazon website.

Jam for Tea by Cathy Murray

Recollections of growing up in the 1950s and 1960s in urban Yorkshire and rural Lincolnshire.

A Single To Filey by Michael Murray

Detective Chief Inspector Tony Forward's hobby is directing amateur theatricals.

His latest production for the Sandleton-on-Sea Players is "The Cherry Orchard".

It's nearly midnight and he still hasn't completed the dress rehearsal. Then duty calls: a man with fatal head injuries has been discovered in a remote bay on the East Yorkshire coast.

The man's name is Mark Coulson and he's the Headteacher of a local primary school. But no-one seems able to explain why this respectable, professional man was at such an isolated spot so late at night. His wife is the most mystified of all.

Why were Mr Coulson's pockets empty? Sergeant Wilmott believes robbery was the motive. But if the killer had stolen Coulson's car keys why is his car still parked nearby?

Was Mr Coulson murdered by a jealous boyfriend or husband? That's what DC Diane Griffiths thinks. But Mr Coulson's Chair of Governors says he was a boring man whose only interest was his work.

With such a baffling case to solve how can DCI Forward find time for "The Cherry Orchard"?

All titles available from the Amazon website.